If In Ruins We Must Live

If In Ruins We Must Live

ISBN: 979-8-9852028-0-9

Ritona

an imprint of RITONA a.s.b.l.
3 Rue de Wormeldange
Rodenbourg, Luxembourg L-6995

Layout and Design: Rhyd Wildermuth

View our catalogue and online journal at
ABEAUTIFULRESISTANCE.ORG

Within

Surrealist Prophecies—7
Put Reason Back to Sleep—11
Tornado Warning—17
Junkyard Nemeton—19
Wage-Slave in the Wasteland—22
The Martyrs—24
The New Sun—26
Metamophosis—29
Caught in the Act—31
Balor Reborn—33
Hold Steady—37
Many Gods, No Masters—39
Now Green, the City—43
Cthonic Poems—45
The Gates of Ys—46
Goetia—48
Mysterium Tremendum—52
Plague Year—58
Wabasha Street After Midnight in Winter—58
Rum and Beer—60
Exiled—61
Solitude—63
Visitation—64
The Bus at Five A.M.—65

Masks—67

Two Men—68

Quarantine—71

Wrath is Coming—72

The Strong Winds Hiss—74

Insomnia—76

Joy—77

Snowstorm in Spring—78

Janus—79

I Never Used a Glass—81

Waiting For a Message—83

The Time is Strange—84

Anger—85

Stranger in a Park—86

We'll Bring The Flame—87

Curfew—89

Siege—90

Poems from Pagan Anarchism—91

Prayer to Our Lady of Anarchy—92

The Wallbreaker Charm—93

To the God of the Wood—95

Millenium—97

To the Goddess of the City—78

"Oh You Mothers"—101

Curse Tablet—104

About—105

Surrealist Prophecies

"It was in the black mirror of anarchism that surrealism first recognized itself." (André Breton)

This is a sequence of apocalyptic prophecies inspired by China Miéville's novel *Last Days of New Paris*, which led me to investigate the Surrealist Manifesto of André Breton and the use of what Breton calls "the magical Surrealist art" as a method of channeling or divination:

> *"Put yourself in as passive, or receptive, a state of mind as you can. Forget about your genius, your talents, and the talents of everyone else. Keep reminding yourself that literature is one of the saddest roads that leads to everything. Write quickly, without any preconceived subject, fast enough so that you will not remember what you're writing and be tempted to reread what you have written."*

The pure "Surrealist game" is unedited automatic writing, but the poems in this sequence use automatic writing only as a starting point—to be followed in each case by many hours of revision and polishing.

The theme of the sequence as a whole is the collapse of our global civilization due to uncontrollable climate change, leading to a mass rejection of both faith and reason and the re-enchantment of our world among the ruins of our failed creations. Some of the poems in the sequence are set before the Fall and portray the spiritual and emotional dilemma of our current crisis. Some describe the Fall itself, and the strange changes in thought and perception that will be needed if any are to survive a world in which humanity has been radically de-centered. Some describe the world to come, a world newly alive with gods and spirits yet free of all dogma or fixed belief – a world of beauty and strange magic.

The first prophecy describes the Fall and prophecies the return of gods and monsters.

The trigger for the writing of the second prophecy was the sound of a tornado warning siren outside the window while reading Abel Paz's biography of Buenaventura Durruti.

The third prophecy centers around Rudolf Otto's concept of the numinous as the immediate presence of the Other, often experienced as a "terrible and fascinating mystery" and described by Otto in The Idea of the Holy as "daemonic dread... the horror of Pan." In "Junkyard Nemeton," an abandoned junkyard becomes a druidic grove as the trees advance, and the numen walks in the reborn forest.

The fourth prophecy explores the horror of living in our world in the last few generations before the Fall, trapped in bare survival as the world begins to slip from its moorings and slide down into strange dreams—a world in which meaning has died and has not yet been reborn. The wage-slave dreams of an apocalyptic wasteland but wakes up to an alarm clock.

The fifth prophecy was inspired by an old CNT-FAI propaganda poster from the Spanish Civil War, and the yearly march in honor of anarchist martyrs every May Day. Respect for our honored dead is not a substitute for building a world.

The sixth prophecy was inspired by an Alley Valkyrie shirt design, and the "rib-caged wreckage" of the Colosseum. It describes the death of a despairing mystic in the years before the Fall, and hints at the coming rebirth of both the individual and the world. The "brass sun" in the poem refers to the failed attempts of the Finnish gods to create a mechanical sun after the real sun was stolen by Louhi, the witch of the north wind. A world without a spiritual heart is a doomed world, and no technology can change that.

In the seventh prophecy, the Change has begun, and the Fall is here. People and buildings assume strange shapes. Reason as we know it is overthrown, and faith as we know it has died as well. The future is limitless—both beautiful and terrifying.

The eighth prophecy portrays the Change itself with gruesome imagery, as people and things assume new shapes. These images are not meant to be taken literally, but make no mistake—the changes we actually face will be equally violent to the world as we now understand it. In the words of a pagan philosopher, "Myth is that which never was, but always is."

The ninth prophecy portrays the rise of the waters, and the washing-away of the great cities. The giants of Irish mythology—the Fomorians, or "undersea people"—are in the rushing of the flood, confident that no gods will oppose them.

The tenth prophecy is placed in the mouth of a survivor, waiting expectantly with a small band of other survivors for the flood waters to recede. The old world is gone, but the shape of the new world is not yet known.

The eleventh prophecy returns to the theme of the first and the warning of the fifth. The world as we know it has fallen and transformed, and the opportunity exists to make something new and better among the ruins. Gods and monsters haunt the city, but there will be no masters in this world. The title is another reference to an Alley Valkyrie design.

The twelfth and final prophecy portrays the world to come, the first generation of the new society. Nature has reclaimed the city, yet people still live there. The world they are building is egalitarian, close to nature and close to the gods. The broken fragments of the old world are all around, shattered statues incorporated into a new mythology. The few who remember what they once represented will never tell.

Put Reason Back to Sleep

"The sleep of reason produces monsters."
(Francisco Goya)

Put reason back to sleep.
Let monsters slip
Out of the corners of your eyes
And lick bricks like meat.
Let them lie them down to breathe
Among the ruins of old useless infrastructure
And there breed new beasts.

The future will have a place for neither faith nor
reason.
But only a fluttering
As of birds in flight
That we can sight in season.
And we can plant new trees in
The broken bones of what we built
While from the silt of dead dreams
We must pick out what still gleams.

The future will have a place for neither fact nor fic-
tion.
There will be no restriction based on creed,
But all eyes will bleed.

From one drop,
A vast bulk
Will heave its hulking tentacles
Up through the holes
In once-solid floors
And splash black ink on broken doors
To announce its presence,
To stake its claim.

Another drop shall bloom
And become a room
Red with blood flowers
Above the flood.
Where we shall
Hold all-night congresses
With the snarled tresses
Of wet hair.
We will carve knots in candles there.

The future will have a place for neither pope nor
king.

There will be no special honor paid to art,
Yet all hearts shall sing.

We will leave offerings at cold crossroads
Where no cars roll.
A strange new song, not a soul.
For the fast unfolding of
Something old.

We will pray quietly in empty stores
Whose floors are strewn with plastic bags,
And weep silently as humbled conquerors
Before shattered windows
To paint new dragons
On flooded streets.

We will hear the gathering of shuffled feet,
The stir of wings.
We will hear the voice
When it sings.

We will praise the flight
Of dead birds
With muttered words
And raise hands in prayer
To sun and air,
To praise the dawn as she gleams.

We'll never ask what it means.
To ask questions
Of either fact or fiction
Is to place restrictions on
Dreams,
And when dreams walk,
That isn't safe.

The gods of the future will not be safe.

For there the ocean,
Now fat and bold,
In the mud-choked memory of some high cathedral
Will hold his revels and make his home.

The sun will dance her way
Through the cracked dome
Of this corrupted capitol
Where cruel laws were made
And pierce straight through it
Like a blade.

And there, death,
Clothed in white,
Will hold court in some aborted

Cinema
And serve drinks all night.

And she who has heard
The merest rumor
Of that old tumor,
Faith—
He who has seen the faintest wraith
Of that old traitor, reason—
They themselves shall have done treason.

For these things bring death.
They taught us to believe
And to not believe
Till there were no gods left.

They themselves brought the dust—
The rust that showed itself as
A red taint in tap-water
And shall become our Fall.

Put faith to sleep.
Let Titans climb up out of the black bowl of your
heart
And squeeze bricks to dust.
Let them lie them down to breed

Among the ruins of old useless infrastructure
And there spread like rust.

The future will have a place for no faith but wonder.
And an endless shattering
Of cracking glass
And a long crash, like thunder.
But we can plant new trees in
The ruined remnants of what we built.
And from the silt of dead dreams
We can pick out what still gleams.

Tornado Warning

A high, proud, howling outside the window through
an enervating lassitude of limp, white streets.

A scar advances across this torn landscape of trem-
bling cheek.

A leak of blood and bone discreetly declares itself
beneath your eyelashes and tells you to wear a pair
of fiery eyeglasses, to declare his reign.

For spring means rain.

And in the swarming bug-storm of divine inventions
there will be no mention of our intentions: what we
made is what we made. This is our one and only
chance: we can dance with the coming sunsets of
oblivion or stay home to sing.

But there is a king: his name is Lludd. They call him
the Once and Future King.

Let us weave a garland of teeth to make his head-
band; let him wear our eyes on his red hands like
rings. This hasn't gone as planned.

And when King Lludd sings,
When the Jacquerie
With brutal mockery
Dethrone and debone
All lesser kings
Oh, when King Lludd sings.

Still if in ruins we must dwell,
Fear not, we shall.
A time for building will come again.

It's not that we cannot build. We built all these
things. The mud-splattered walls of all your flooded
palaces, the brick-battered glass facades of all your
callous palisades. We built all these things.

And we shall know how to dwell in the shell of the
world you made us make for you before we build
our own.

Junkyard Nemeton

Dead cars and broken plastic crates with empty bottles bloom.

Roots twist and turn while weird lights burn, out there beyond the gloom.

Discarded wedding rings and books, lost toys and headless dolls.

The forest grows and no one knows what comes and goes, what calls.

There's something there, with tangled hair. It walks, and drips, and moans.

The song that calls me to the night sounds sweeter than my own.

I step across the muddy ditch and jump the broken fence.

Between the trees, the night-owl sees, and flees in self-defense.

I raise my hands in recompense and mutter words of prayer.

Strange laughter fills the junkyard night. I whisper "who is there?"

Novitiate, initiate, at last I shall be shown.

The lies that brought me here tonight seem truer than my own.

I lived my life in constant strife, in service to a creed.

But here at last I have no past, for here there is no need.

I stepped across the border and I crawled across the wall.

Here reason sleeps and faith retreats. The forest eats them all.

I'm startled into silence by a long and lonely moan.

The truth that called me here tonight seems stronger than my own.

Ten thousand years now disappear. In some forgotten time,

My ancient dead here bowed their heads as I am bowing mine.

This forest, or another forest - forests without end.

As faith retreats and reason sleeps those times shall come again.

I speak, but I could never tell the things that I was shown.

The words that I would need are so much stranger than my own.

The wings that flap, the eyes that see, the creatures with their call.

The mountain past the forest looms - strange, black,
and fat, and tall.

The birds, like gods, are eating flesh. Skulls guard
the cave of bears.

Nine-fold the numen walks tonight, and dogs are
howling there.

In polar coldness, near the heart, flame flickers on a
stone.

The star that leads me to the light is brighter than
my own!

Wage-Slave in the Wasteland

Between life and death there is just a breath, pluming out like choking smoke in the cold cracked morning of "not much left."

Some part of me dreams...

Between life and death there is just a breath in the fresh anger of the frozen morning. Bare bushes burn in a dustland of rusted cars. My eyes stare out across the flat plain and coolly assess if there might be rain. A train approaches, black puffs of coal smoke chugging out angrily into the autumn air. There is a dead dog there, crawling along on broken legs with mindless eyes before the tracks. The scene lacks color, lacks contrast. The air feels thin, but leaves a slick film of grease on the skin. The sun looks parched, fighting to create its own conditions for some new existence that might pierce these clouds. Munitions cook off in the distance with a breakfast crackle as a castle burns.

Some part of me yearns...

But between life and death there is not much differ-
ence. A sick horror, and stuck tears. A body ex-
hausted from all the acid years, corroded to almost
nothing, holed-up like cheese. A red alarm demands
full attention and announces that the morning now
pounces upon you with its sharp intentions. The
numbers flash, and you crash down from the
grotesque fantasies of forgetful sleep to keep faith
with cash. Dustland dreams disappear — another
morning, another year.

We live here in the wasteland in which the Grail
once shined, with no question on the tip of our lips,
our gestures false like mimes. The fisher king was
never healed, they never meant for us to heal him.
They only meant to conceal what we'd been fed, so
they concealed him. And what was revealed when
they pulled the cloth away was just his worm-wet
head.

Alive or dead? Too many days beneath this airless
mystery where no soul has history, tied fast to the
bedpost of this harsh necessity. I can no longer tell.
And worst of all, I'm not even sure I can still recall—
was I alive before? Was there, at some point, more?

The Martyrs

Outside, the waters of a springtime sky
Plunge screaming from the heights.
And in the stain
That creeps along this poster on my wall
Free Barcelona falls.

And on the rain, I hear dead heroes asking if they
lived in vain— if there was no message in their mar-
tyrdom, no future hope, but only a longer rope with
which to hang ourselves.

To clinging altar cloths, to cluttered shelves,
Our selves attach themselves.
Adore your gods,
But never tell yourself your faith can change the
odds.

No cluttered shelves with hanging altar cloths will
ever save us. Nor will any ancient yellow poster of
some killer angel explain the stain of sin or let us in

on the secret of how Christ forgave us and how at
last our cause must win.

Our gods are here—
They move within our bodies and the turning of the
year.

Our gods are real—
They live in every drop of blood and every spark of
wood or steel.

Our dead are dust—
Unless we give them life with every act, in each of us.

Our dead are seeds—
These flowers never bloom with faith
But deeds.

The New Sun

Instructions for a funeral—
Hold no tribunal.
That man was a gnostic,
If often caustic.

So make a new sun out of brass.
Bless it with burnt cash slipped from the pockets of
the old Caesar
Who drools in his glass castle counting calculus,
And tell the fire I'm coming soon.

If you want to, sweep my room.
Croon if you need to, but do not keen.
Nobody asked me to shake my fist at archons,
If you know what I mean.

You know I was never one of those clashing cymbals,
Hollow of throat like a brash jackal.
I never brayed at any tomb.

And if I sang
A wordless song sometimes
Beneath the stars and moon
To unseen powers
And you ask what for—

Well, I was only waging war.

I wasn't fond of flowers.
Gather up
Whatever broken coffee cup
You considered "ours,"
And tell them all
My time had come.

If it feels numb, don't poke it.
Just rinse your eyes out completely,
Comb your hair out neatly,
And go home.

But as for me, I'll be gone.

For empires crumble as I've been told,
And in the rib-caged wreckage of gray leviathans
I may glimpse some hint

Of the blueprint of this shared corruption.
I may come to comprehend why I could never mend
My own desolation.
I may erase my station.

My eyes may become the starry skies
That are not wise nor foolish
But only real.
My cuts may heal into healthy hillsides
Of humming bees.
My blood may flood.
My breath might bloom.
There are a million things I might become.

And in some life—
Some life I cannot imagine,
Some distant life—
I may look out beneath strange skies
And there glimpse your eyes.

Metamorphosis

The seasons turn—the beating of a wound.
Time gushes out and splashes on the floor.
We tacked a blanket up
But that's no more.
The light comes creeping
Through the crack beneath the door.

And in the summer sun my eyes have begun to run
like half-cooked eggs. I sense the waving of a spider's
legs, the buzz of bees, the weirdly ticklish feeling
stealing slowly upward toward my knees...

All signs announce,
The change has come.
I will be something other
Than I started from.

I have become a meal for hungry stars
That burn as red as wine and walk the shifting line
Of mine and yours.

Don't close the doors.
And leave those windows open too.
The change we tried to hide from has arrived for me
and you.

And in the thick, wet heat my skin has begun to peel
and pull apart above my heart, while in the street I
hear the flapping slapping sound of altered feet.

All laws retreat,
All buildings crack.
Faith crashes into reason at high speed
And kills them both on impact.

The broken compact splits my bones.
My ribcage spreads and cracks, my slit lips groan.
From deep inside my body
Something rises
Something moans.
Something alien and lovely
Lifts it head to see its home.

Caught in the Act

Caught in the act of giving birth
To a new oil-paint earth of no set design,
You will lie there dying.

This hundred-year brick building, sick with death,
Will pulse like the breath of a vermillion flower, slick
and wet,
The thorns of which will twitch with passion -
Bloodied marble, passion spent.

Carved chunks of fat and meat
From feet and arms
Shall hang from every road-sign, drawing flies.
You will stare, unmoved.
Your eyes will show no surprise.

Like clinging vines the lines of flesh
Will hang stretched as if from hex to hex,
The spread-out skin and fat
Of some exalted wretch.
He will stink of sex.

Like broken beauties,
Here dismembered,
Streaked with tears,
You will bleed and bloom.

A god will rise in beauty from your tomb.

Balor Reborn

A dim and distant roaring,
Then a crack
Like branches snapping
Then an awe-struck hiss
Of indrawn breath
Without a chance to scream.

As thick as melted chocolate,
Foaming mud
With rocks and chunks of concrete
Crushes walls,
Cracks windows open,
Carries cars away
And levels all our works
But leaves the wrecks
And skeletons of structure
Here and there.
The air is filling up with hungry birds.

The rushing waters of the sunless sea
Have broken past the borders
And have born
The bloated bodies of the newly dead
Like bobbing corks
Along the roaring stream
With mattresses
And bottles,
Plastic bags,
And cardboard boxes.

Waters of the deep,
In lightless caverns
And the great abyss
You made your home.

Oh, giants of the deep,
You sleep no longer.
Stronger than the chains
The gods once forged
To keep you from the sun
With mighty cries you've come.
And in the rain
As waters rise
Your eyes will shine again.

34

Our cities,
Once bright jewels on the plain
Are swept away
In shards of shattered glass
And buckled girder.
In the rending shriek
I hear the one-eyed king of giants
Speak:

"My name is Balor.
In another age
I marched against the gods
In pride and rage
And fell, defeated
By a flying stone.
I died that day,
But I was never gone.
Since long before
Your people walked the earth
I've known that I would know
A second birth
In rising oceans
And in fiery sun.
My eye is open,
And your time is done.

No skillful god shall come
To cast a stone.
My name is Balor.
I shall rule alone."

Hold Steady

Hold steady. The hints of a new life are ready to poke gray fingers up between the cracks in the sidewalk and burst straight out through this chalk graffiti. Don't be too greedy. We are not yet sure. Let the waters recede a little. We will then know more.

The floods have come. We are no longer what we started from.

Hold tight, hold fast. The level is dropping slowly, but what's past is past. The last of the old world still must rot. The last of its thought.

Hold steady. The hints of a new life are ready to poke gray fingers up between the cracks in the sidewalk and bloom green and bright.

We must survive the nigh—and all the other nights. We must survive the flood. We must not just survive but thrive in mud.

From mud reborn. From blood and fire. From
flooded halls and broken bits of fallen walls we must
conspire.

The world is new. It need not take the shapes it took
before for me and you. Don't be too hasty. We are
not yet sure. Let the waters recede a little. We will
then know more.

Many Gods, No Masters

Now monsters pull their bodies,
Dripping wet,
Through manholes
From the depths
While others rise
With open eyes
From drops of blood and sweat.

They drip down faces,
Splatter on the street,
Then rise, congealed
To lick the walls like meat.

And here among the broken bricks they'll breed.

Now reason finally sleeps.
Now faith retreats.
For those who cling to either,
This is hell.

The ocean rises
And the cities swell
With mold and water
Stinking in the heat.
And giants walk on wet and ancient feet.

The broken bones of all our art and pride
Lie rotting in the tide.
All eyes now bleed.
Without a church to specify a creed
Each drop becomes a seed.

A heaving bulk
With sodden hulking grace
Lifts up its face
Its tentacles unfurled
And shrieks its challenge
To the brave new world.

A red splash blooms.
In sagging walls
Of dripping, black-stained rooms
Blood flowers bloom,
And candles flicker bright.

So yes, we'll pray tonight,
We few who live.
Yet none will beg for life.
And none will give
A penny or a thought
For what we lost.
That ocean has been crossed.

Though gods have come,
These gods do not forgive.
Nor do they judge.
They neither save nor damn.
They bear no grudge.
Each one declares "I AM"
And nothing more.
And we must do the same.

Our gods are flickers in the spreading flame
The roaring of the water
And the light
That plays along these ruined walls
At night.

Our gods are real.
They live in every drop of blood and every spark of
wood or steel.

Our dead are dust—
Unless we give them life with every act, in each of us.

Our dead are seeds—
These flowers never bloom with faith
But deeds.

This world is not the world it always seemed.
It's time to make the world of which we've dreamed.

No god shall rule,
No king,
No man shall rule,
No giant either.
There are many gods,
Too many now to count,
Yet none shall rule.
We're done with ruling
And with those who rule,
With what they built
And all their useless tools.

This city has become the land of fools.

Now Green, the City

Now green, the city is a nest of vines
Twined-up like snakes
And climbing toward the stars
Through open windows
Up the walls of banks
As if to offer thanks.

On elephantine branches, in the night,
We gather close
To hear each other sing.
We have no priest.
We have no sacred king.
Our songs are songs that
Everyone can sing.

New oaks poke out below us in the street
Where water runs
Around the lopped-off feet

Of some historic general
Whose head
The children painted red.

They know him as The Giant, and believe
He came to eat our flesh
And crack our bones
Before our singing turned his flesh to stone
And left him down there,
Broken and alone.

The moon comes out.
We shout in wordless praise
And hold each other close beneath its rays
While someone pours an offering of ale
And tells the glorious tale.

Now green, the city grows,
And like the leaves
Our children grow.
And no one ever grieves
For who The Giant was or what he did.

If there are any left here who could tell
They keep that secret well.

44

Cthonic Poems

The Gates of Ys

Half a nation drowned by water,
Half consumed by fire.
Those who profit, smug with laughter,
Fear no prophet calling "Liar!"

Ash comes floating from the heavens,
Storms come rolling in.
Preachers close the doors of churches,
Calmly fold their hands, and grin.

We who listened, we who bargained,
Now praise God in sheer despair.
Gods like fire and wind and water
Do not heed such prayers.

Sorcerers of coal and oil,
We invoked, they came.
Never mind the prayers and praises,
Last-ditch rages, guilt and blame.

Gods as deaf as us have gathered:
Storm and flame and wind.
Now the gates of Ys are opened.
Now the ocean rushes in.

Goetia

To the tune of "In the Pines"

I will moan
I will moan
I will moan
I will moan
Dressed in rags, and my hair will be down.
Oh, you spirits in flight
Ride on moths through the night
And alight at the top of my crown.

Now my head with their dead dreams is swarming
I am not what I was, I can tell.
By the price I have paid
And the magic I've made
I will go on a voyage to hell.

I will go
I will go
I will go

48

I will go
On the sea of the whispering dead
With a wreathe on my brow
And a head on my prow
And a crown for the murmuring head.

And the crown will be made out of iron
And the eyes of the dead they will burn
And the head will proclaim
All their barbarous names
So the gates will swing wide
In their turn.

I will sing
I will sing
I will sing
I will sing
As I walk through the ash and the rain
By the mountains of glass
Made of dreams that have passed
And the bones of the giants in chains.

Oh, their blood with the starlight is seething.
When I drink of it, I will be dumb.
In my silence I'll weep

For their dreams in the deep.
In my sorrow for what
They've become.

In the kingdom below, there are regions -
Some of fire, some of ice, some of stone.
There are oceans of mud
There are rivers of blood
There are forests of hair and of bone.

There are spirits sublime and most subtle.
There are others both vulgar and strange.
There are spirits who fly
Through the underground sky.
There are others who burrow and change.

If you wish to be allied with legions
And to know all their names and their signs
You must enter your mark
In the book, in the dark
You must drink of the fire and the wine.

I will moan
I will moan
I will moan

I will moan
Dressed in rags, and my hair will be down.
Oh, you spirits in flight
Ride on moths through the night
And alight at the top of my crown.

Mysterium Tremendum

Originally Published in "A Beautiful Resistance: Everything We Already Are"

1

Hot ashes sizzle on the rocks and snow
While high above me, hunting falcons glide.
A single strand of grayish smoke still curls
Like twisting rope against a huge, white sky
So cold it shocks the last thin threads of dream
And leaves me clean and startled and awake,
Though cold, and frightened by my coldness too.
The foothills stretch behind me, nearly bare,
But pocked with lonely, black-white scrubs and birch,
And broken here and there by boulders too
Like naked hands that grasp the empty skies.
I pour a stream of steaming water out,
And orange coals go black with veins of fire,
Then fade to gray. I heft my leather pack,

Which holds a bare few odds and ends, and stand.
This land is haunted by a howling wind,
That whistles like a steam train through the hills
Then blasts across the white and empty plains
And drives a cloud of snowdust, thin and dry
And glittering like shards of ground-up glass
Through barren branches. Though the road is long,
There's nothing to be gained by staying here.

2

The white light fades. And all around, the wind
Seems hushed for just a moment. Then it roars.
A sheet of crystal dust springs up and roams
Half-drunkenly from hill to hill. I stand
With eyes cast down, and feel the hostile kiss
Of ice against my face. I look again
And find myself alone. My heart is bleak
With such a wind as this. I face the path
As if its outline mapped the wasted track
Of all my years. But then I shrug, and walk.
The hard, bright snow that breaks beneath my boot
Shines white as distant galaxies. The storm,
As predatory as those passing birds
Seems somehow not to touch me. I am dead,
And wrapped in distance like a shroud. The world

Must have its reasons, but my reason fails.
I set my face against the harsh, white scream
Of primal winter, and set forth again.
Through spiral clouds of wind and shards of ice
Like shattered glass, my solitary path
Is marked behind me by the shape of boots,
Ahead of me by nothing. In this wind,
My thoughts themselves seem hushed, then torn
away.

3

The path ahead is packed, hard, crusted snow
Through which a single, withered clump of grass
Pokes up its pale green head. The air seems clean
And charged with life like static, and I breathe
A lung full as my feet break through the ice
To sink into the snow beneath. Ahead,
A wrathful, orange sky. The clouds, like thoughts,
Change constantly and pass. And in their train
Ride intimations of a flood of ghosts.
Before me stands a circle made of stones,
An ancient holy place once sanctified
By blood and fire, now by wind and time.
Nine stones in all, nine gray and twisted stones
Nine long forgotten, cold, ice-crusted stones.

54

This place is of the Other, and the face
Of utter silence shines behind and through
Like shifting lights behind a veil. I kneel.
Mysterium Tremendum, how your great
And awful gnosis penetrates my being!
In such a place as this the changing years
Are all retained at once. My heart is still
Before the fearful mystery I've found.
In hushed yet pregnant reverence, I breathe
The magic in from every silent rock
And frozen pool of water, and I know -
A god is here behind the rock and ice.
The gods are here, and we are not alone.

4

It's time to drink the clear, cold wine of dream
Directly from the source, and know its tang
As well as any ancient poet knew
The flavor of the dawn songs of the world.
Our bards have drained the wells of story dry
In singing odes to nymphs they never knew
Except through pages in a well-worn book -
And now no longer sing of nymphs at all.
Our priests have done the same with every creed
They once assured would save us from ourselves.

Our scientists have chopped up every truth
In bloody chunks of fact, and then announced
That all they found was meat. The world is dead
Because we chose to kill it. But the gods –
The gods are here, and we are not alone.
Real magic's not a thing you go to learn
In books of lore like dried-out yellow bones.
It's not a thing that you can get in school
By sitting at the feet of wise old men
And letting them dissect the things you've read
To make a mess of symbols. Myth is awe!
Real myth will leave you shaking on the ground
In love with every speck of earth, alive,
And all alive with you. It's time to rise
In holy rage and wreath your head in lights
You've plucked yourself until your eyes, ablaze,
Illuminate the world. It's time to learn
New myths directly from the land of dreams
And plant those myths like seeds in every rock,
In every rushing stream, in every hill,
In every city, till the whole world blooms,
Until the whole world comes alive again.

Plague Year

Wabasha Street After Midnight in Winter

The shovel scrapes along the broken street
And half-awakens me. My eyes are shut,
It's after midnight, and in booted feet,
Whole teams of men are working while my gut
Is scraped by something just as dull as what
They scrape the sidewalk with. Or so it seems.
At forty-seven, all we want from dreams

Is that they last the night. And all we get
Is some fresh twist on why they never do.
One night a loud, performative, drunk, threat,
The next —and just as loud —"I love you too."
On other nights the street is softly blue.
Men stumble by, then stop a while and sing
As if that 40-ounce had crowned them king.

It's not as if I don't recall the taste—
That half-free moment, belting at the stars!
One night is like the next, and I won't waste
The breath to criticize. The passing cars
Have places where they need to be. The hours
Must all be filled with something, no mistake.
Some men must shovel, some must lie awake.

Rum and Beer

Spiced rum and dark, brown beer – the hours slip by
As loud and fast as laughter. You with tales
Of lovers lost and unregretted. I
With slightly fearful stories of the trails
On which I lost my way. The words pour out
And fill our glasses, foam up on the rim,
Then stain our shirts. You slap your knee and shout
With honest joy. And yet my eyes go grim.
I note the time politely and suggest
It might be getting late. You nod, agree,
And shake my hand goodbye. It's not the jest
That spoils the mood, but only when we see
Behind the dark brown tint of rum and beer
The shadow of each heavy, snow-hung year.

Exiled

Ride in silence through the night,
Staring out as cars go by.
Watch for nothing. At the sight
Close your eyes and wonder why.
Wonder why they never told you,
Those who tried and failed to hold you,
That years
Like fears
Wear down all locks and break all gears.

Off the bus and in the street,
Walking for an hour or two.
Hands in pockets, soaking feet –
Waiting for a thing to do.
As the ice beneath you glistens
Wonder why you never listened,
And why
Your eye
Would seem to fade when they came by.

Walk on streets without a sign,
Stand on corners till the dawn.
Pour an offering of wine,
Drink up the rest. And on and on.
On some bench in grim December
Take a moment to remember –
You said
Instead
That you would rather end up dead.

Solitude

I fear
The coming year.
Each jagged part:
The winter is the start—
For months I'll shun
The dim, forgetful sun.
For months I'll close my door,
And I'll remember nothing more.
Then spring shall come again
And I will roam the streets like other men

But I
Will soon go by
Unheard, unseen,
And faceless as a dream.
When summer's here
And fountains flow so clear
That birds hop up to drink
I'll sit and watch, and I will think.
Then stand, and turn, and go
To wait the wind that brings the coming snow.

Visitation

On Friday night, I take
My coat and hat, a pair of gloves, and go.
I walk through thin, wet snow
And watch the shapes the passing headlights make
In deep, brown pools of water.
A thousand miles from here, the biting wind
Would snap and nip my skin.
A thousand miles from here, the winter cold
Would feel as mean, as old...
But I would lose my daughters.
As I approach, both children grin.
I stop, and smile, and pull them in.

The Bus at Five A.M.

I came here from a life I'd lived so long
That leaving almost killed me. I was wrong
In every bone, in every pulsing vein.
The streets, at five a.m., cast such disdain
In my direction that I could not face
The looming buildings of this strange new place,
And so I'd walk while staring at my feet.
Slick ice on every sidewalk, every street
Conspired to make me slip. I'd creep along
Through deadly wind while whispering a song
I only half-remembered. Then I'd wait—
A pair of eyes behind a scarf —and hate
The things they'd done to me, and what I'd done
To earn this half a life. And as the sun
Came creeping up, I'd catch my bus, and go.
I'd ride in silence while the falling snow
Became a kind of mud outside. The cars
Would crawl, with headlights on, by shuttered bars
And darkened storefronts while their drivers cursed
Their lives, their jobs, the whole damn universe.

And when the bus pulled in, I'd step outside
And stand there waiting for the second ride
I'd have to take to get to work that day.
The wind would shake the signs and blow away
A used-up bag or rattling, empty can.
And none would speak—no wasting, dead-eyed man
Or angry, silent girl. I'd watch the sky—
The clouds that passed, the birds that floated by—
And wonder who I was. Why was I here?
A year ago—one solitary year—
I had a home, a wife who held me close,
Two girls who loved me. Now I was a ghost
Who haunted bus-stops, silent and alone.
Unseen, un-mourned, forgotten, and unknown.

Masks

Those who've lived a dozen lives
Lose the sense that they've survived.
Building lives becomes a task:
How to paint a lifelike mask.

How to make your essence clear,
How to make the eyes appear.
How to hide, and how to show
Only what you'll let them know.

And they'll buy it, more or less,
Sympathetic and impressed.
Smiling, they will play along,
Not one word will strike you wrong.

Even so... there's something here.
Hints of falsehood, hints of fear.
Are they wearing masks as well?
If they were, how could you tell?

Two Men

The wind was blowing sharp and cold
With bursts of stinging rain,
When, feeling tired and stretched and old
I stepped off from a train.

I meant to catch a bus, and so
I had no time to spare.
The rain came down. I tried to go.
A man was standing there.

His eyes were not a killer's eyes.
They shone with pain and fear.
But with that look, not dead nor wise,
Of many an awful year.

He lifted up a trembling hand
And softly blocked my way.
And all that I could do was stand
And let him have his say.

He pierced me with his eyes, so grim
They seemed to strike me down.
I stood in place and looked at him
While the rain fell all around.

"You have to understand," he said,
"I do not want to kill...
But if they mean to strike me dead,
Well, then of course... I will."

I saw those eyes, I saw that gaze
And my mind went down the track:
Ten-thousand half-forgotten days
Till a thought came slowly back.

Of how my friends and I once faced
A man whose eyes were grim.
He stepped so proud into our place
But we took his pride from him.

He swung a heavy, drunken hand
But I ducked, and knocked him down
And then, like dogs, we swarmed that man
And kicked him on the ground.

Near thirty years have passed, and I
Can still recall his screams.
The shrieks of those who wandered by,
The blood that ran in streams.

Now here I was, in stinging rain,
And a cold and bitter wind.
This man was reaching out to me
In sorrow, pain, and honesty,
And I knew that I had sinned.
Though thirty years had passed, yet still
I knew that I had sinned.

"Go home," I told that haunted man,
"Go home and go to bed."
He whispered, "yes, I understand,"
Though his eyes were filled with dread.

And then he dropped his hand, and I
Walked on into the night.
The rain kept pouring from the sky
And yet my steps were light.

Quarantine

The sun is out, and birds fly here and there.
The wind feels cold, but strangely clean.
The streets are bare,
The people gone. What could it mean?
The winter fades at last, but everywhere
We bar our doors. The city holds its breath.
That silence that you hear
Is just our fear:
Four million people hiding from the thought of
death.

The joyful, hungry birds—
It's like they haven't heard.
Likewise the wind and sun.
All things on earth now make the spring
Except for only one.
And every living thing
Now flies or swims or makes its nest.
The world awakes, but mankind takes
A silent and a fearful second winter's rest.

Wrath is Coming

1

The sky is bright, but gray. A hint of light
Shines, flickering, behind the clouds. Outside
The streets are silent. And a hint of night

Comes creeping slowly up these clean and wide
But not quite empty streets. A man walks by.
With eyes like death, he looks from side to side

Then bellows, "Kill them all!" We hear his cry
In rooms where we've been locked inside for days,
But no one looks. He screams, "They have to die –

"I'll hunt them down! I'll kill them all!" He stays
Beneath my window for a little while
Just screaming out his challenge. These are days

When mental chaos breaks the heavy, still
And fatal silence of the city's will.

2

And someone answers. Driven by his fear
Or foolish pride, he takes his stand and yells:
"You shut your mouth! Go on, get out of here!"

Then total silence reigns. In all the hells
Where we have locked ourselves, we sit and wait
To find out what the man will do. The bells

Ring out the hour. And thick with rage and hate
His voice rings out as well. "They have to die!
For wrath is coming!" Like some mindless fate

He rolls along. The echoes of his cry
Play back his words. He stalks along the street
Still shouting out his prophecy. And I

Cannot deny a certain strange appeal.
For even rage can cleanse, and wrath can heal.

The Strong Winds Hiss

The raindrops splatter on the city streets and the
cars splash through
like violent birds diving for a meaty fish.
There are voices somewhere, distant voices, one
raised in fear and anger.
The strong winds hiss.

A crackle, a burst of lightning, the thunder stutters
and the window creaks.
There are voices out there, like a distant murmur, a
song I can't remember...
And the strong winds hiss.

The puddles scatter like exploding fireworks as the
cars blast through them
and the strong winds hiss.
There are voices out there in the wind and weather,
like a life I cannot remember.
And the strong winds hiss.

Out there on the streets, the raindrops splatter.
The cars splash through.
I will not go out, for the streets are unfriendly.
The air here is poison.
I am poison too.

The lightning crackles across rain and rooftop, and
the boom of thunder... like giant feet.
In our rooms we huddle, in our rooms we wait.

Whoever is out there, I wish them no harm.

The thunder stumbles across a wounded city, its
laughter unpitying, its laughter great.
In this world we huddle, in this world we hide.

The voices distant across a shuttered city, their pain
unfixable, their hate like the sea:
In depth unguessable, in wrath unknown.

Out there on the streets, the raindrops splatter.
The cars splash through.
I will not go out, for the streets are unfriendly.
The air here is poison.
I am poison too.

Insomnia

I'm waiting here behind a bolted door —
Two days have gone.
I lie in bed, observing every hour—
And watch the sun.

It crawls across my wall, then slowly fades
And goes to black.
I watch the night's cacophony of shades
Until it's back.

The morning comes, the air is slow and thick
A new day creeps
And drags itself, disgusted, weak, and sick
But never sleeps.

Joy

Where can I find the joy I used to know?
It made me stop once on a rain-slick street
And laugh, delighted, lighter than a leaf
Blown high on spring's first breeze. It made me sing
In every tongue in which I knew a song.
It made me smile as if I was a door
And opening to say "please come on in,
We're glad to see you." And it made me love.
But that's the trouble. Joy can set you free,
But love can catch you in a grief so strong
You'd rather suffer than know joy again.
My children, for example. When they cry—
And not because of some mere bump or bruise,
But when they sob out with the hurt of life—
It stabs my bones, my flesh. That is no joy.
And yet I'd rather suffer, side by side,
To comfort them, to help them in their need,
Than laugh with joy for all my life to come.

Snowstorm in Spring

Snow.
Even so,
Though the window shows a white chaos
There is no sense of loss
As in the slow dying of the Fall.

All
The old walls
Of this brick city are crusted white.
Down on the street, the night
Is all but silent. Then the wind shifts,

Lifts
The snow drifts
And playfully batters them. The storm
Feels welcome—almost warm.
For, after all, it will soon be gone.

Janus

I've lived this life between.
Not one, but two.
My feet have walked in dream

And stepped in blood.
I've flown so far
I know the music of a distant star,

And I have slept in mud.
Two lives I've lived:
One, unforgiven, haunted by a sound—

The high-pitched, birdlike scream
Of human fear,
One free, and high, and clear.

I've climbed the peaks
And seen high mountains
Shining white with snow.

I've stalked
The watchful menace
Of a late-night walk

Through hateful streets.
With eyes I've watched.
With cold eyes I have watched

These lives of mine.
And after all these years
I still can't say which life is true and real

And which is just a mask.
Its only task:
Obscure. Deceive. Conceal.

I Never Used a Glass

I never used a glass, back then.
I raised a bottle, though.
The cheerful faces of my friends
Shone brightly even so.
Till 3a.m. we'd drink and talk
Then take our early morning walk

Through all but empty streets to find
A place to serve us food.
It wasn't just the sweet, red wine
That made our laughing mood.
Now all those days are past and done,
And of those friends, I've kept not one.

Time eats away at everything,
My world is wearing down.
And those who'd talk, and drink, and sing,
I wonder where they've gone.
Such nights of words and wine were they—
But all those things have passed away.

I never use a bottle now.
I drink wine by the glass.
And those who laughed, and showed me how,
Have faded like the past.
I take a sip and think of them—
My lost but unforgotten friends.

Waiting for a Message

My nerves, electric, seem to hop and skip.
They jump like dying fish. I check the phone
And find no message. Yes, I'm well aware,
No message is expected. I am hooked
On such a jagged barb I cannot twitch
Without a spike of pain. I sit as still
As if I slept. The hours crawl weakly by
On broken knees. How is it that this life
Can paralyze all joy and leave it stuck,
Like mud encrusted in a rusty pipe
Where once clean water flowed? How is it we
Can end up crippled by the needful things
That once brought laughter, open smiles, and
peace?
I check the phone again. There's no release.

The Time is Strange

The time is strange. And troubled too.
The city streets are almost bare,
And anyone who wandered through
Would say, "there's no one living there."

The windows watch beneath the stars
Like staring eyes though still and black.
No sound except the passing cars.
No feeling but this aching lack.

Behind those cracked and fading bricks
Are people, though. All hid away,
The well, the ill, the getting sick,
They wait the coming of the day

With mixed emotions. Some will thrive
And some will suffer. Some will die
And some will have to stay alive
When all is lost. Which one am I?

Anger

Their eyes were wet with tears that wouldn't fall.
More frightened of my pain than of their own
They almost whispered, "No, that isn't all.

I'm angry with you sometimes." With a moan
They wrung their hands together as the thought
Escaped their lips. And seeing that they'd shown

Their inner self, they twisted in a knot
Until I kissed their forehead once again.
"That's always how it is. You know, you ought

To show your father anger now and then.
I'm just a man, and wrong like other men."

Stranger in a Park

We sat together in an empty park
And watched in silence. Everywhere the dark
Was rising as the sun went down
On such a wounded, such a sickly town.
I didn't say a word, and nor did you.
You only came because I'd asked you to,
And there was nothing, nothing left to say.
I heard a sound and looked along the way
To find a man approaching with a mask
Across his face. As if he had a task
And meant to do it, he came rolling by
And parked his chair across from us. And I
Then broke the silence. "What's he doing there?"
You shrugged as if to say you didn't care,
Until he pulled the trumpet out. And then
He played a long and lonely note. And when
We heard that note he played, I shook my head.
"He's here to mourn for us." That's all I said.

We'll Bring the Flame

It isn't fog. It creeps along the street,
A blanket, white as mist. The sound of feet
Comes marching in behind it, and the fear
Spreads out ahead. And then the first, sharp tear.

It isn't fog. It's like a low, flat cloud
That hovers sinister. And then the crowd
Starts running while the flashbangs crackle, flash
And boom like thunder. At the snapping lash,

I run as well. My eyes run wet and sting.
My friends are somewhere up ahead. A sling
Swings out and casts a chunk of brick. We run,
Into a world where there is now no sun

But only burning whiteness. There's a crack,
A burst of light, a hurt man on his back.
Glass shatters, somewhere close. I hear their feet:
The sound of Law advancing down the street.

It isn't fog they march behind. This mist
Spreads out its fingers. If we still resist
They'll choke us with it, and we'll get the blame.
You brought the tear gas. Now we'll bring the flame.

Curfew

Behind a wall, and all the lights out there
Are staring at us. Trapped, we do not dare
To show our faces. Hiding in the park
We wish the night was deeply, truly dark.

It's after curfew, and the soldiers walk
These streets of ours. We hear them as they talk.
Their rounds are live. We don't know what they'll do.
We have to find a way out, that is true,

But fences rise behind us, and ahead,
Those rows of lights. I cannot feel the dread.
The only thing I know that I can feel:
The strange conviction that all this is real,

More real, in fact, than me. We turn and run,
In furtive silence, crouching. One by one
We fade like echoes lost among the trees.
And no one shouts, for no one even sees.

Siege

I'm crouching on a porch. The street below
Is almost empty, but the hungry glow
Of passing headlights, like the eyes of sharks,
Comes floating by. A distant burst of sparks
Illuminates the city, and a boom
Comes rolling down the street. A sense of doom
Hangs hot and thick. Three sharp, repeating shots
Crack suddenly nearby. Tonight, my thoughts
Are strange and watchful. And tonight, my face
Holds no emotion. Sitting in its case
The rifle at my feet is silent too.
We watch the street. There's nothing else to do.

Poems from Pagan Anarchism

Prayer to Our Lady of Anarchy

A poem inspired by Ex-Voto's "Madonna dell'Anarchia"

Oh black-robed lady with the bleeding eyes,
Red-belted, standing on an open book,
With hands outstretched but empty. Hear our cries!
In dread and sorrow for the things you've seen
You weep for us. And yet your heart is fire.
Oh red and black Madonna, let desire
Come blazing through us till we cannot sleep.
Destroy our apathy
And help us keep
Our covenant with rage,
Our own bright fire.
And let our eyes bleed with the same desire
Until the day arrives when we shall see
Fulfillment of the prophecy
That someday soon, a flood
Shall cleanse these streets and wash your cheeks of
blood.

The Wallbreaker Charm

a spell for breaking barriers and enclosures

Wild powers of the earth and air,
High walls have risen everywhere
And where we once in common held
The woods and fields, now trees are felled
To fence us in on every side
And satisfy the greed and pride
Of those who buy and sell it all.
But something doesn't love a wall...

Power of earth, cast down these stones
And shatter them like splintered bones.
Power of air, come blow them down
Until they're broken on the ground.
Power of fire, burn out these walls
Until the structure sags and falls.
Power of water, rage and flood
And sweep away these walls with mud.
Power of ice, build up so thick

You bend and buckle every brick.
Power of lightning, fast and just,
Blast walls apart and leave them dust!

Not merely walls of wood and stone
That close us in. Not walls alone,
But all enclosures you can find
Of wood or plastic, word or mind
Intended to enclose or fence
Our open space. In recompense,
Oh earth and wind and fire and flood,
I offer you, not smoke and blood,
But something dear to gods and men -
The chance to be yourselves again.

To the God of the Wood

Will you meet me in the thick wood where the shadows shine and the sunlight falls so thin it leaves no record on the wind?

Will you walk in the tall trees where the whispers walk, where I've heard you wail?

Will the fury of a sudden breeze make your name a crazy call?

In groves where light can never reach will you become the sound of birds?

And when my silence is my speech, will you remove my need for words?

God of the woods, with the laughing eyes, you are a world of pale stars in a purple sky beneath the wildness of the night.

You are the tears of the dead bards who whispered
sadly when you smiled; you are my years of wasted
words—so come and walk with me awhile.

Dark-haired, bright-eyed, drunken god, your hard
face, your beastlike walk- our world has grown to
need your grace. It is no longer time for talk.

Though in your eyes there is no time, or world, or
sight, but only space; though hints of holy rage and
crime distort the joy that lights your face,

Yet hearts are known by what they love and peoples
by the creed they serve—and this time more than
any time should have the god that it deserves.

Millennium

Black birds come screeching through the skies
On winds of war, as waters rise.
And prophet's eyes begin to gleam
Beneath their floating hair. This dream
Of smoke and fire shall end at last!
A whisper rises from the past –
Millennium—as pillars shake
Millennium—as gods awake
Millennium—as flowers bloom
In mouths of corpses, and the tomb
Springs open to reveal the Host
Arranged for battle, ghost by ghost,
With banners flapping, black and red.
Millennium—"We are the dead
Who rose with Spartacus and fell,
Who sang John Ball Has Rung Your Bell,
Who marched with pitchforks on Versailles,
And those who answered Boukman's cry,
Who rode with Makhno in Ukraine,
And those who died defending Spain.

We are the dead of all the earth
Who died to bring this day to birth.
The dead who dreamed another world
Have come to you with flags unfurled.
The burning wheels and turning gears
Have come around. The end is near.
Our work remains undone. But you
(Millennium!) shall see it through.
So take your mental spear, and go!
Cast down all thrones. Let forests grow
Where burning mills once filled the sky
With smoke and flame. Let empires die,
Till none is slave and none is king.
Then heal. Then build. Then sing."

To the Goddess of the City

In wooden beams, in bricks, in cobblestones
I see your face and feel your watching eyes.
And when the alleys moan
With wind I hear your cries.
You dance in every shaking sign
And drink when gutters run with spilled red wine.

You slip unnoticed in your all-night walk
Through empty playgrounds marked with fading
chalk.
You sleep on benches in the winter cold
Forever growing old.
You see all secret things, and know all crimes
Committed on your streets. And you reveal
All things the wicked wish they could conceal.

When paper skitters down an empty street
At 3AM, I hear you walking past.
And I can hear the echoes of your feet

In sirens and in breaking glass.
Protect all those you pass along your way
And see them through until the light of day.

Oh goddess of my city, I am poor.
Keep hunger from my family's door.
Protect my neighbors from the storm
And keep us all well-fed and warm.
And I, in gratitude, will do the same
For others, in your name.

"Oh You Mothers..."

*This is the prayer I use when leaving offerings for
my own ancestors.*

Oh you mothers, all my mothers
Those who sleep in heavy soil,
Those who went to death so weary
All you thought was no more toil,
Those who danced with joy and laughter,
Those who fought to break the chains
Though you'll know no more hereafters,
Here a part of you remains.

Oh you fathers, all my fathers
Those who dream in wet, black earth,
Those who let their dreams go hungry
So that mine could come to birth,
Those who died in rage and sorrow
Those who laughed and wandered free,
Though you'll know no more tomorrows
Your tomorrows live in me.

All of you who came before me,
Though I know your names or not.
All who added to my story
Giving blood or deed or thought.
Take this food and drink I give you,
Share it with me, take your fill.
Though your verses may have ended
Yet the song continues still.

Curse Tablet

I write these words on sheets of lead
And leave them in a dead man's hands
To bring them to the silent lands

Of root and water, and of rot.
I whisper them into the ear
Of one who can no longer hear.

I show them to the gaping eyes
Of one who lies beneath the leaves.
Oh gods of dread who punish thieves,

Leave off all lesser punishments and hear!
The thieves who rule the world have gorged
On others' bread and meat. They've forged

New manacles to bind the wrists
Of any who resist. They kill
Whoever will not do their will.

Oh gods who dwell beneath the earth,
Arise tonight and hunt for prey
More worthy of your power. Slay

The kings of thieves, the lords of men,
And not the poor who steal their bread.
I write this curse on sheets of lead

And leave them in a dead man's hands.
I whisper them into the ear
Of those who sleep, but always hear.

I show them to the empty eyes
Of those who lie beneath the leaves,
Oh gods of dread who punish thieves!

Christopher Scott Thompson

is an anarchist, martial arts instructor, and devotee of Brighid and Macha. He is also the author of *Pagan Anarchism* and *The Book of Onei*.

Ritona

Ritona is an imprint of Ritona a.s.b.l.// Gods&Radicals Press. Named for the Treverii goddess of river crossings, we are a non-profit publishing organisation advocating for plurality, tolerance, and respect for Pagan, Indigenous, and non-industrial ways of being in the world.

Find our online journal and book catalog at ABEAUTIFULRESISTANCE.ORG